WHAT CATHOLICS BELIEVE

In 20 Lessons

by
John Redford

*All booklets are published thanks to the
generous support of the members of the
Catholic Truth Society*

CATHOLIC TRUTH SOCIETY
PUBLISHERS TO THE HOLY SEE

CONTENTS

INTRODUCTION

To the Instructor

1. These notes were written week by week as I gave a course in the Catholic faith to a young person who came to me for instruction, and so were not intended originally for publication. But, if any priest or catechist finds them useful in instructing those interested in being introduced to the Catholic faith, then they will indeed serve a useful purpose, well beyond what was originally intended for them.

2. It must be first remembered that this course is not 'do-it-yourself', and can in no way be considered adequate without an instructor. Each week's lesson - the course comprising twenty weeks in all, 30-45 minutes per lesson - is only an outline; and the instructor will have to 'fill in' and explain each of the points made.

3. It will be helpful if your enquirer has prepared the week's lesson in advance, so that he is ready to ask questions and discuss points arising from the notes.

4. As time goes on, the enquirer may be given additional reading material, if he or she wants it. It is a very good practice for the instructor to have a good amount of books

and pamphlets which can be handed to the enquirer as
required, to take away, read, and, hopefully, return!
People will differ very much as to reading capacity, and
this course can be given without any other reading being
done, if the instructor judges that the enquirer is not the
'reading type'. But obviously, the more interest shown in
good reading material, the better.

5. At the close of the course (Lesson 20) there is a series
of questions summarising the course. Where the first
enquirer who did this course was concerned, these
questions were asked by me without prior warning, since
a memory examination would surely serve little purpose,
and one wanted to find out how much had really gone
home, without any 'swotting'. Needless to say, the
instructor could well compile a questionnaire of his own,
tailor-made to his own enquirer's needs. But for some
enquirers, to feel that questions can be answered at the
end of a course may well be most encouraging.

6. Just as this course needs an instructor, a priest or
catechist, to work at all, so it must also be emphasised
that it is not intended to be a complete expression of the
Catholic faith, only an introduction to it. It is to be hoped
that, if, after this course, the enquirer is received into full
communion with the Catholic Church, the instruction will
still continue, at least to the extent that the instructor sees

the newly-reconciled Catholic from time to time (perhaps once per month during the first year) to discuss problems, and to find encouragement in the growth of Christian life. The instructor should perhaps be especially concerned to see that the new member is beginning to feel a part of his new-found family, God's Church.

7. Finally, different enquirers will find different questions to ask; some will have problems concerning marriage and family life, some with questions of faith, such as God's existence or the truth of the Gospels, others with problems concerning justice and peace in the world. It is therefore again the skill of the instructor to develop parts of this course as those questions arise. And, if the inadequacies of this course start you writing another of your own, so much the better! The instructor has the vital task of communicating the Gospel of Christ to his enquirer, of being an instrument of the Spirit of Truth. May he use you effectively for this purpose.

1. 'I HAVE CALLED YOU FRIENDS'

1. Friendship is the most important thing in life, apart from our own life itself; and even if we stay alive, our life is not worth living without friendship. Loneliness causes the greatest suffering (e.g. broken marriages, children leaving their parents, friends betraying each other).

2. People spend a lot of time therefore trying to make friends whom we can rely upon and love, and even try to buy friendship, but without success. Friendship begins and continues because one person is attracted to another, and loves to be with that person. In particular, this is true of marriage, which is one of the deepest kinds of friendship which we know on this earth, and where two people vow to spend their lives together until death.

3. The Catholic faith is about God and ourselves becoming friends. Jesus Christ, the Son of God, said to his disciples, 'I call you friends, because I have made known to you everything I learnt from my Father. You did not choose me, no I chose you...'

4. Our deepest loneliness is caused by the fact that we are not born 'naturally' to be friends of God. Not only is God invisible to our eyes, but we often get the feeling that we

have done things which do not please him. The story of
Adam and Eve in the Book of Genesis tells us of how
mankind originally lost God's friendship by not doing
what God wanted, in fact by disobeying him. Therefore,
just like human friendship, man loses his friendship with
God by doing what God does not like. Again, Jesus said
to his disciples, 'You are my friends if you do what I
command you...'

5. The Christian faith, then, is the story of how God went
out of his way to restore the friendship which we had lost
by disobedience. God has shown us how we can restore
that lost friendship, and the Catholic faith shows us how
to live a life of love and friendship with God through his
Son Jesus Christ, beginning in this life and ending never!

6. But what do we have to do even to start becoming
God's friends?

(a) Believe that God exists. Although we cannot see him,
we know that God is there because an infinite Spirit is the
only adequate explanation of the creation of the world as
we know it. He must exist because we exist. He is
therefore our 'father' and we his 'children'.

(b) Commit ourselves to follow in his way. He has shown
us how to become his friends in the Bible and in the Life

of the Church. We simply say, 'Lord, I want to be your friend always; teach me your way, and I will try with your help to follow'. In that way, we can never go wrong.

(c) Talk to God our Father, and so become his friend. This is what we mean by 'prayer', the development of our human relationship with our heavenly Father. That is why Christians say regularly the prayer his Son taught us.

Further discussion

Discuss friendship and how we respond to God's friendship. Discuss and learn the 'Our Father'.

Scripture references

1.3 John 15:15
1.4 Genesis chapters 2, 3; John 15:14
1.6 (a) Romans 1:20
    (b) John 14:6
    (c) Matthew 6:9-14

2. THE OLD RULES

1. Although we all find any rules irksome, we yet have to admit that some regulations are necessary if human life is to be peaceful and well ordered (e.g. 'Please keep off the grass' is a regulation intended to keep the grass in good condition for everyone to enjoy).

2. Rules are generally put in a negative way ('You may not park your car on double yellow lines') in order more clearly to mark off the forbidden area. However, even if the law is expressed in a negative way, its aim is always positive, for the benefit of everyone (double yellow lines forbid traffic to park, but only in order for all cars to move more freely down that particular road).

3. When God first chose a people to become his special friends, he had to educate them away from the customs of their neighbours, who murdered out of revenge (as the story of Cain and Abel tells us), and even sacrificed their children to their gods in order to win their favour. He needed, then, to impress their simple minds with his power and with his truth. (And we, perhaps, are not so different today).

4. God, therefore, first showed the Israelites how powerful he was, but only as a means of attracting them

to himself. He allowed them to become slaves in Egypt, and then helped them to escape miraculously from the power of the Pharaohs across the desert. He then led them into what they called the 'promised land', 'a land flowing with milk and honey', the land of Israel, in which land they were to live according to his rules, and so to begin to become his friends.

5. Now, we all know that no friendship can be founded simply upon a set of rules; there needs to be love as a solid basis for a personal relationship. But on the other hand, we also know only too well that there can be no friendship between two people where one is harming the other by cheating or continually lying. Like any good set of laws, therefore, God's old rules simply told his people the limits beyond which they could not go if they wanted still to be called his friends.

6. Christians have now been given a 'new law', the Spirit of God's love poured into our hearts by Christ our Lord. But the old rules given by God to Moses are still important to us, because they express the voice of our own conscience telling us right and wrong. John the Apostle said, for instance, 'How can a man say that he loves God if he hates his brother?'.

7. Here, then, are God's old rules, the 'Ten Commandments':

You shall have no gods except me
(Our duty is to honour God alone).
You shall not make yourself a carved image
(God is invisible, spirit).
You shall not abuse the name of God
(We must respect God, and revere him).
Remember to keep the sabbath day holy
(One day per week for rest from work).
Honour your father and your mother
(We must love and care for our parents).
You shall not kill
(Life is sacred, because man is made in God's image).
You shall not commit adultery
(Marriage is a sacred covenant).
You shall not steal
(We must respect other people's property).
You shall not bear false witness
(It is wrong to slander another's character).
You shall not covet
(That is, lust after what belongs to someone else).

8. Now a prayer to ask God to help us to keep happily in the way of his Law: Almighty God, you are all light, in you there is no darkness. Let your light shine upon us in all its radiance, so that we may walk gladly in the way of your commandments. Through Christ our Lord. Amen.

Further discussion

Discuss the need for rules and laws.

Scripture references

2.2 Genesis 4:1-16; 1 Kings 16:34
2.4 Exodus 3:7-12
2.6 1 John 2:3-11
2.7 Exodus 20; Deuteronomy 5

3. WAITING FOR THE MESSIAH

1. We all know that waiting for something or someone increases the delight when the event actually happens, e.g. birthday presents, preparing for holidays. Half the pleasure is in anticipation. This pleasure is even greater when a person is involved whom we love, and whom we have not seen for some time. In this case, we are not merely 'waiting', we are 'longing' for that person to come, and to make us happy with his or her presence.

2. What we call the 'Old Testament' is the time of waiting for the Messiah, Christ, to come (about 2,000 years from Abraham's time to the time of Christ). The Jews had to wait this time, because they had a great deal to learn before they were ready to receive the Messiah; and indeed, as we know, when the Messiah did come, only a chosen few of the Jewish people (such as Mary, the Apostles, and Paul) recognised him, just as all through their history, only a few had recognised the prophets as coming from God, those few being called 'the remnant'.

3. The word 'Messiah' means 'Anointed', the ceremony of anointing being the old way of crowning the king, or consecrating the prophet. David the king, indeed the greatest king in the history of Israel, was called the

'Messiah' because he was anointed king by the prophet Nathan. And God promised to David that his son would always be king in Israel. Thus, in time of trouble, the Jews began to look for a Messiah, the son of David, who would once more rule them in justice and in peace.

4. What were they expecting the Messiah to do for them?

(a) He would be a good shepherd, a better King even than David. He would help the poor and the weak, and defeat all their enemies. In his time, even the animals would be at peace with each other.

(b) He would be an ideal Priest, not relying on animals offered and slaughtered, as with the sacrifices of the Old Law, but offering his own sufferings to God for the sins of the people. He would say to God, 'You don't want sacrifices; I am offering myself'.

(c) He would be an ideal Prophet, not only telling people that they had disobeyed the Ten Commandments of God's Law, but helping them to change their hearts by giving them the Holy Spirit of God, so making them want to follow God's way and become his friends.

5. In the Catholic Mass, after the introduction when we confess our sins to our heavenly Father, we always on

Sundays have a reading from the Old Testament. In this way, we join the Jews of Old, waiting for the Messiah to come, and, together with them prepare for his coming. In this way, also, we prepare ourselves better for the Gospel reading, where we hear of the words and deeds of Christ, and finally to receive our Lord in Holy Communion.

6. Then, again at Mass, after the Reading, we say 'This is the Word of the Lord', indicating that we believe that God is speaking to us; and we follow by saying or singing a Psalm, one of the Hymns of the Old Testament, to praise God for speaking to us in the Old Testament, and to join the company of people waiting for the Messiah. Just before Christ came, there were many Jews so waiting for the Messiah, even a community of monks on the Dead Sea at a place called Qumran. But the most famous man who waited for the Messiah was a man called Simeon, who, when he held Jesus Christ in his arms, said this most famous Christian prayer:

Now, Master, you can let your servant go in peace, just as you promised; because my eyes have seen the salvation which you have prepared for all the nations to see, a light to enlighten the pagans, and the glory of your people Israel. (The 'Nunc Dimittis', or 'Song of Simeon'; sung at Night Prayer).

Further discussion

Why is the Old Testament important to Christians?

Scripture references

3.2 Micah 5:1-6
3.3 2 Samuel 7
3.4 (a) Ezekiel 34:23-31
    (b) Psalm 40:6; Isaiah 52:13-53:12
    (c) Deuteronomy 18:18
3.6 Luke 2:29-32

4. A Boy is Born

1. The birth of a child is perhaps the happiest of all human experiences. We see the wonder of new life, the helpless dependence of the tiny infant on its mother, and above all the great love which the parents have from the beginning for the child which is the fruit of their own love.

2. When we read the story of Christmas, the birth of Christ, in the Gospel of Matthew, and the Gospel of Luke, we capture once again the joy that Mary, Joseph, and their relations and friends had at the greatest birth of all time; and we should share their joy, because for us, just as much as for them, Emmanuel, God-with-us, is born.

3. If part of the wonder of birth is the wonder of new life, then the birth of Christ is still more amazing, since Christ is truly the Son of God, and so, in the Christian belief, God becomes a tiny infant, for us. This is why God chose that Jesus should be born of the Virgin Mary, and should have no human father, Joseph being only Christ's 'guardian' as the husband of Mary. The true father of Jesus was God the Father, whom Christ always called 'Abba' (Dad!).

4. However, although having no human father, Christ had a human mother, and depended upon her in every

way while an infant and a child. This was because Christ had come to save us from sin (the word 'Jesus' means 'Saviour'), and to create the love of God his Father in us. To do this, he began by creating the love of God in his own mother Mary.

5. This is why Catholics have a great devotion to Mary, his mother. When the Angel Gabriel came to her and told her that she was to have a son, she made a great act of faith. Be it done to me according to Your Word; and so began a relationship with God's own Son which was so deep that she became, in God's eyes, the greatest of all creatures, apart from Christ himself.

6. Little is known of Mary's life apart from what we read in the Gospels. We believe that, in order to be a fitting mother for God's Son, Mary herself was free entirely from sin, and remained so till the end of her life on earth, when she went to join her Son again in heaven.

7. Mary is, therefore, an example of a perfect Christian life; she loves us personally as our mother, since we are children of God, and Christ is our brother; and finally, as the greatest of the 'saints' (i.e. those who have gone before us to heaven), her prayers to God the Son are most effective for us, her spiritual children.

8. Catholics, then, do not treat Mary as an idol, but as the beginning of God's love story, who can help us as a human being in our journey. Above all, she is the girl of humble origin who became, by virtue of her faith, hope, and love, the 'Queen of heaven', the first sign of God's victory over the devil.

9. We speak to Mary, therefore, with love and devotion as our mother, and ask her to help us develop that deep relationship with her son that she always enjoyed. We begin with the greeting of Gabriel:

Hail Mary, full of grace, the Lord is with Thee; blessed art Thou among women, and blessed is the fruit of Thy womb Jesus. Holy Mary, mother of God, pray for us sinners, now, and at the hour of our death. Amen.

Further discussion

Why do Catholics have such a strong devotion to Mary? What is the difference between devotion to Mary and worship of God?

Scripture references

4.2 Matthew 1:18-25
4.3 Mark 14:36
4.4 Matthew 1:21
4.5 Luke 1:38

5. JESUS OF NAZARETH

1. Of all the great personalities who have ever lived, and even among the great religious leaders in this world's history, perhaps Jesus of Nazareth is the most famous. What the centurion said at the foot of the Cross, 'This was truly a good man', is the verdict of anyone who reads the Gospels.

2. But Jesus himself would not have been satisfied with merely our approving of him. He called disciples, that is, people who were to follow his teaching. And these disciples were to share his way of life as a travelling herald of God's kingdom. They were so attracted by the powerful and loving personality of Jesus that they were willing to sacrifice everything for him.

3. The first thing which attracted so many people was the healing power of Jesus. In contrast with John the Baptist, the announcer of the Messiah, who told them that they were wicked sinners and must flee from the wrath to come, Jesus began by healing sick people wherever he went, and particularly by curing the possessed from their madness. In this way, he showed his power over all the forces of evil, and his love and pity for suffering humanity.

4. The second thing which again attracted thousands of Jesus' own contemporaries was his magnificent teaching to huge audiences in the open countryside. They were struck by the power and authority of his message, and by the fearless way in which he criticised the hypocrisy of the religious leaders of his time, and welcomed the outcasts of society, encouraging them to make a new start with their lives.

5. Central to the teaching of Jesus was the idea that, in order to please God, we have to do more than simply obey the Ten Commandments; we have to get to the spirit of them, which Jesus expressed as the twofold command of love; to love God with all our hearts, and to love our neighbour as ourselves. And there are no limits to this love. For instance, Jesus said it was not sufficient just to say 'Thou shalt do no murder'; it was also wrong to destroy people's dignity by insulting them, or by failing to help them.

6. But Jesus was not just a great teacher. He wanted people to ask themselves the question 'Who is He?' Among the disciples, Peter, a fisherman from Galilee, seems to have had the awareness fairly early on that Jesus was no ordinary man, particularly when he saw Jesus was able to calm a storm, and find huge catches of fish when all the fishermen had given up. But, more than any one

thing which Jesus did, was the sense that he gave to Peter of God's presence; and so, when one day Jesus asked the disciples, 'Who do you say that I am?', Peter answered, 'You are the Christ, the Son of the living God!'

7. When we become the friends of Jesus Christ, therefore, we become friends of God, because Christ is the Son of God, God become man. However, the disciples did not see this very clearly before the death of Christ and his resurrection; even when they saw a vision of Christ in glory on mount Tabor, together with the old prophets Moses and Elijah, they still did not understand.

8. Above all, the disciples could not understand when Christ spoke to them of the necessity of dying at the hands of his enemies. Everyone knew that Jesus had made enemies by his outspokenness and as a result of his enormous success. But where the disciples went wrong was to assume that their leader would use his power to defend his position. They were soon to realise, however, that his way, and their way, was to be the Way of the Cross, and so to the victory of love.

Thank you, Lord Jesus Christ, for all the benefits you have given me, for all the pains and insults you have borne for me. O most merciful Redeemer, Friend and Brother, may I know you more clearly, love you more dearly, and follow you more nearly, day by day. Amen.

Scripture references

5.1 Luke 23:47
5.2 Matthew 4:18-22
5.5 Matthew 5:20-48
5.6 Matthew 16:16

6. FATHER, FORGIVE THEM

1. To forgive the harmful things which people have done to us is perhaps the most difficult thing for any human being to do. And forgiveness is that much more difficult if we love (or loved) the person involved, because the hurt is that much greater.

2. No one loved the human race more than Jesus Christ, because he loved us with the love of God, as God's Son. And no one did greater good for the human race in healing their sicknesses, and preaching the Good News of God's love. Therefore, the crucifixion of Christ as a common criminal (the most painful death invented by the cruelty of man) was the worst injustice ever perpetrated by the human race.

3. It is all the more amazing, therefore, that Christ was prepared to forgive his persecutors, who were jealous of his success, and fearful as to the consequences if the movement started by him grew too large. But in this, he was giving us an example as to how we should behave as Christians, forgiving those who harm us.

4. Christ knew quite early on in his ministry that he would die on the Cross. That is why, just before his arrest, he

celebrated the Passover (a Jewish festival supper commemorating the departure of the children of Israel from Egypt) with the disciples for the last time on earth. But, instead of the usual sacred meal, Christ took the bread and wine and said, 'This is my body, this is my blood, poured out for the forgiveness of sins', thus celebrating the first Mass, and showing that the forgiveness of sins in his name continues for ever now in the church.

5. But he showed this forgiveness even more clearly to all men when, on the cross itself, instead of cursing those who had unjustly murdered him, he said to his Father in heaven, 'Father, forgive them, because they do not know what they are doing', saying the same words of encouragement to the robber also on the cross with him: 'This day you will be with me in Paradise'. But not only the people around him on that afternoon were forgiven; God the Father accepted Christ his Son's deepest prayer in his agony on the cross, and forgave us all because of Jesus' love and forgiveness.

6. However, not all accepted his forgiveness. Judas went out from the Last Supper, the first Mass, and committed suicide in despair. Even worse, some of the people watching Christ crucified only mocked him, and dared him to come down from the cross. It is possible for people to be very hard and to resist the love of God.

7. Jesus eventually died, and was buried in a new tomb bought by Joseph of Arimathea, a wealthy Jew who supported Christ during his public ministry. But, early in the morning, some women, including Mary Magdalene, came to anoint his body, only to find the tomb empty. 'He is not here, he is risen', they were told.

8. Christians believe that Jesus appeared to his disciples, and ate with them, in order to prove to them that he had risen from the dead. Then he breathed on them the Holy Spirit, to give to them the power of forgiving sins for all those who were sorry, and who would promise to try to live better lives in the future. Thus, by his resurrection, Jesus proved finally that he was the Son of God, since he had power over death; and he proved that God answered his prayer, 'Father, forgive them', by saying, 'Yes, I do forgive'. Now an old prayer of Eastern Christians:

Lord, Jesus Christ, Son of God and Saviour, have mercy on me, a sinner.

Scripture references

6.3 Matthew 5:43-48
6.4 Mark 14:22-25
6.5 Luke 23:34; 23:39-43
6.7 Luke 24:6

7. HE IS RISEN

1. The experience of death is the most frightening of all that we go through as human beings, because it is truly a leap into the unknown. Thus, of all the subjects which we talk about, death is the least popular as a topic of conversation. But we all know that one of the few certainties which we have in this life is that we will die and so from time to time we venture to think about it.

2. The greatest fear regarding death is that it is in reality the end of our existence, when we return to 'nothingness'. However, it is here that the Christian hope is strongest, because we believe that death is not the end, but the beginning of a new life, where we shall be with God for ever, and 'every tear will be wiped away'. In this way, for the Christian, death is not only something to look forward to, but is also a motivation for living, because we know that everything which we do on this earth has a purpose, to prepare us for eternal life with God.

3. Even before Christ came, the Jews were growing in their faith in the 'after-life'. They, and Christians too, do not only believe in the 'immortality of the soul', but the 'resurrection of the body', that is to say, the resurrection of the whole person of man, which includes in a mysterious way body and soul.

4. Still, no one, not even his closest disciples, really believed Jesus when he told people that he would rise again from the dead after his crucifixion and death. It was the women who found his tomb empty on the first Easter morning, and the disciples did not believe them. The 'empty tomb' for the Christian is a sign that Jesus had risen from the dead, both body and soul, since, if only his 'soul' lived on, his body would still have been there; unless, of course, someone had stolen it, which the Gospels strenuously deny.

5. But even the 'empty tomb' was not enough to convince the disciples that Jesus had risen. He had to appear to them, speak to them and eat with them, for them to believe; and Thomas even had to touch the wounds (or at least was challenged to do so by Christ) before he would say, 'My Lord and my God'. Thomas in this way acts on our behalf; because he saw, we believe without seeing.

6. The appearance of Jesus to his disciples also emphasises that the resurrection of Jesus is not simply his resuscitation, his recovery from death. It means that his whole person has been transformed into a new kind of existence, eternally to be with his Father and praying for us, offering his whole life, death and resurrection as a perfect sacrifice which the Father accepts willingly.

7. And that is why the resurrection of Christ is the most important event of all in the whole story of our salvation. Eventually, the appearances of Jesus, which were only to convince the disciples that he had risen, ended, and the Lord 'ascended into heaven', to be present with us now by faith, and by the coming of the Holy Spirit. He was with his disciples briefly, to tell them that he would be with them until the end of the world, through the Spirit and through his body the Church.

8. For the Christian, the resurrection is not only something to look forward to at the end of the world as we know it. Christ before he ascended into heaven breathed his spirit on the disciples, and so upon us all through them. And this means that there is new life within us, the life of Christ, which is constantly against our old ways, the 'spirit of death', until, after our actual death, this new life is completely liberated, as it was when Jesus, 'the first fruits from the dead', left that tomb empty with the stone rolled away.

Acclamation at Mass:

Christ has died. Christ is risen. Christ will come
again. Alleluia! (A Hebrew word meaning
'Praise Yahweh', Yahweh being the old name
for God in the Old Testament).

Scripture references

7.2 Revelation 7:17
7.3 2 Maccabees 7:13-14
7.4 Luke 9:22
7.5 John 20:28
7.7 Matthew 28:16-20

8. THE CATHOLIC CHURCH

1. We all realise how much we depend upon each other, from the time when we are helpless babies dependent on our parents completely, to old age when we need everything to be done for us. But even in our healthiest moments, we need the guidance and help of others to make life more worth living. That is why we have the State, the family, the school, the club, the gang, the team; and the Church.

2. We believe as Catholics that Christ founded the Church; that he intended us to live as Christians as one body, not 'doing our own thing' in isolation from each other. That is why he began his Church by calling 'disciples' (learners), twelve chosen men, who were to share in his mission. He depended on them, and they, even more, depended on him. They went around with him, learning his teaching, using his power to cure the sick, and preaching his Gospel.

3. Their leader was Peter, whom Christ called 'the Rock' on which he was to build his Church. Christ wished his work not to cease after his death and resurrection, but to go on from strength to strength; and Peter was to be the leader in this new work, in spite of his weakness and

unworthiness. Thus, on the day of Pentecost, it was Peter who preached the sermon, saying that the Holy Spirit of God has come to take Jesus's place, and that all men of any race, could accept that message, and have the comfort and help of God's spirit in their lives.

4. Thus the Catholic (universal) Church was born, under Peter's leadership, and grew enormously, in about twenty years covering almost the entire known world.
Peter went eventually to Rome, and handed on his ministry to his successors there, the Bishops of Rome (whom we call the Pope, i.e. Father). Although all the Popes are unworthy of their task, they have the help of the Holy Spirit to be our leaders, to teach us the truth of Christ, and to be the final court of appeal on difficult matters.

5. But Peter could not do this work all on his own. He needed the help of the other apostles, and particularly of Paul, who had a vision of the risen Christ while he was going to Damascus to persecute Christians. Under Paul's brilliant missionary dynamism, the Church eventually had more Gentile members than Jewish, since so many were hungry for God and the pagan religions did not satisfy them.

6. However, the Church did not consist only of its leaders, great though they were. From the beginning,

people of all walks of life became members of the Church, and even the smallest had something to contribute. St Paul likened the Church to a body, where each part has its function. We do not all have the same part to play in the Church, but we are all equally one people in Christ, and there is no place for racism in the Church, or for feelings of superiority.

7. The central message of the Church is that God has forgiven our sins, and made us once more his friends. This is most of all expressed in the sacrament of baptism, which makes us Christians and gives us God's life. But it is also expressed in the sacrament of penance (turning from self to God), which exists to forgive sins committed by baptised Christians, and particularly serious sins against the Ten Commandments as given their meaning by Christ our Lord. We come to the Church, represented by the priest, for forgiveness, because sin is not only against God, but against our fellow-Christians as well.

8. But the Church does not exist only negatively to forgive our sins, but to give us the new life of God. This is why we must now turn to consider the sacraments (the holy mysteries) of the Church much more closely. They are acts by which God shows us personally his love, and by which we show him our faith and love in return.

Further discussion

Discuss our need to have community with others. What do you think of the present Pope? His succession from the Apostles?

Scripture references

8.3 Matthew 16:18; Acts 2:14-36
8.5 Acts 9:1-19
8.6 1 Corinthians 12:12
8.8 John 21:17

9. BECOMING A CHRISTIAN

1. People often ask, 'What is a Christian?' In this day and age, they will often give a moral answer to this question, to the effect that a Christian is one who loves his neighbour, and helps everyone he can. In saying this, they have expressed a most important and vital aspect of Christianity, that we must all try to live as Christ himself lived. They should say of us as they said of the early Christians, 'See how these Christians love one another'.

2. This is all very true. But there is still more to being a Christian. Surely people of other religions (Moslems, Hindus, etc.) also try to love each other just as Christians do? There is then, something more to Christianity than a code of conduct; it is first and foremost a life of faith.

3. From the beginning, anyone who wished to become a Christian had to be baptised, that is, bathed or washed in running water as a sign of God cleansing from sin. Thus everyone who wishes to become a Christian must first of all recognise that he or she is unworthy of God's love, and has deserved to lose his friendship, both as an individual and as a member of the human race.

4. But to say that we are sorry is not all we have to do in order to become a Christian. We must believe that Jesus is the Son of God, because, in believing this, we are led to love him as the Son of God, and so are filled with the love of God. There is no true love without faith, faith in the fact that God's Son loves us, and has come down to earth to show us the true way to the Father.

5. That is why, at every baptism service, there is a profession of faith by the candidate; and even when a tiny infant is being baptised, his parents have to make the act of faith for him, until he is old enough to make it personally. And that is also why we say the Creed, the act of faith, at each Sunday Mass, to make us realise that this act of faith is not something which we do once and for all, but need to do throughout our lives.

6. A Roman Catholic Christian is one who believes that being a Christian also implies accepting the Pope as the successor of St Peter, and accepting the continued guidance of the Catholic Church as to matters of faith and moral conduct. Christ said to his apostles that 'the Holy Spirit will guide you into all truth' and to Peter, 'Simon... I have prayed for you, that your faith will not fail'. This does not mean that we condemn other Christians to hell-fire; but it does mean that we believe that the Roman Catholic Church is the Church which

Christ founded, and which is prevented by the Holy Spirit from teaching what is false.

7. At baptism, the Christian promises that he will renounce evil in all its forms, and will try to live a life which is as close as possible to that of Christ himself. This, of course, is impossible on our own; and even the best of us often fail. But in this we have the help of Christ given to us in the Sacrament of Baptism, and he has said, 'Lo, I am with you always, even to the end of the world'. So we must believe that, having begun the life of a Christian we will, with Christ's help, persevere to the end of our life on earth.

8. To help us persevere, we have the Sacrament of Confirmation, which gives us the strength of the Holy Spirit in our daily lives. This also helps us to play our part in the community of God's people as Christ's own apostles. Ways in which we can play our part will be considered later in the course; but we all have our own contribution to make, as members of the body of Christ.

A Prayer to the Holy Spirit:

Come, Holy Spirit, fill the hearts of your faithful, and kindle in them the power of your love. Send forth your spirit, and we shall be recreated; and you will renew the face of the earth.

Further discussion

Look through and discuss the rite of Baptism and the
Confirmation service.

Scripture references

9.1 Acts 16:31
9.3 Acts 2:38
9.4 4 John 20:31
9.6 John 16:13; Luke 22:32

10. THIS IS MY BODY

1. There is no more important human activity than eating, without which we would soon die. But meals are also family and friendly occasions, where our sharing of food is a sign of sharing each other's lives.

2. Meals are also sacrifice because we always eat other living things, whether plants or animals. They die, in order that we might live.

3. This is why, from very primitive times, the most important forms of worship have nearly always been associated with the sacrifice of animals and even human beings, followed by a meal (and even sometimes by the sprinkling of the blood of the victim of the sacrifice) to show solidarity not only with each other, but with the god we worship. The death of one means the life of many.

4. In the days of the Old Testament there was an elaborate system of sacrifice carried on in the sacred Temple. However, the prophets were always complaining that the people tended to think their sacrifice would be accepted by God if they obeyed the ritual; whereas, the prophets said, the true sacrifice accepted by God was not rivers of blood, but a humble heart and a promise to try to live a better life in the future.

5. There was an ancient belief in the Old Testament that God would accept the sacrifice of the people if it was offered by a 'just' man, God's servant, a man who obeyed God's law completely, and so was acceptable to him. This just man, we believe as Christians, was Christ our Lord himself, who as we have heard already, lived a life of complete conformity to the will of the Father, of love of God and man.

6. Just before he died, Jesus celebrated a final meal with his disciples, the meal called the 'Passover' in which a lamb was killed and eaten by the Jews to remember the great night when they escaped from Egypt where they were slaves. Instead of the lamb, however, Jesus told them that in the future they were to feed on his own body and blood, the new sacrifice and the new meal for Christians.

7. Catholics believe that, when Christ said the blessing over the bread, 'This is my body', and then the blessing over the cup of wine, 'This is my blood of the new covenant', he wasn't only speaking in a parable, but that he really meant it to be taken literally. This is what we call the doctrine of the Real Presence, the belief that Christ is really present in the sacrament of Holy Communion.

8. This is a great mystery, because the bread and wine do not change their appearance at all. But what it means is

that Christ becomes present to us as our food and as our drink; without himself of course suffering in any way, since his sufferings ended on the Cross when he offered his life finally to the Father in sacrifice: 'Father, into your hands I commend my spirit'.

9. And this is why, for the Catholic Christian, the Mass (an old word meaning 'dismissal' or 'mission') is the most important part of our faith; as the old saying goes, 'It's the Mass that matters'. In Holy Communion, we become united to Christ, and to each other. And that is why it is important for us to go to Mass each Sunday, to share in the sacrifice of Christ, and to take Christ as our food and drink in union with each other, on the 'first day of the week', when he rose from the dead.

As we receive Holy Communion, we can prepare by saying the following:

Soul of Christ, make me holy: body of Christ, save me; blood of Christ, fill me: water from Christ's side, wash me; may Christ's passion give me strength; O good Jesus, hear me!

Further discussion

Look through slowly and discuss Eucharistic Prayer III. Discuss the experience of going to Mass.

Scripture references

10.3 Leviticus 1; 23:26-32
10.4 Micah 6:6-8
10.5 Psalm 51 (the 'miserere')
10.6 John 6:52-71
10.7 1 Corinthians 11:23-32

11. THE TWO SHALL BECOME ONE

1. Love is as strong as death. The Song of Songs, part of the Old Testament, tells how powerful is the force which draws man and woman together to get married, to give themselves to each other completely, body and soul, to the end of their lives.

2. The first attraction is physical, since man, as part of the animal kingdom, shares in the animal desire, implanted in us by God, to extend the species and so to enlarge the human family. The Church never condemns this strong physical attraction of man and woman, but on the contrary sees it as part of God's plan for the human race.

3. However, all of us realise that we cannot found a human relationship which is going to be stable purely on physical attraction. Desires and emotions are fickle, and can change even from day to day, let alone during the years. What we think is 'love' might only turn out to be 'lust'.

4. That is why one of Christ's most important sayings was concerned with marriage. In reply to the Pharisees, who accepted divorce and re-marriage in certain circumstances, Christ shocked them by saying that if a man divorces his wife and marries another, then he

commits adultery: 'whom God has joined', he said, 'man must not divide'.

5. For this reason, the Catholic Church will never allow two Christians who have married to divorce and remarry (although in certain circumstances it may be better for them to live apart from each other for a while). This is because, in the words of the Bible, the 'two have become one'.

6. For many people in this day and age, such an idea is quite impossible; but that is to see the matter without faith, without hope, and without Christian love. The idea of Christian marriage is that ordinary physical attraction should grow and develop into love which is Christ-like, following Jesus who loved us even though we were unworthy of his love. Marriage, like any other relationship, will have its ups and downs, its joy and its crosses; but all can contribute towards our growth in the love of Christ.

7. Marriage, then, exists in the Christian view as a holy mystery, as a means whereby two people come to find Christ together in their daily life. That is why the marriage service takes the form of a 'sacrament', a vow where Christ seals the promise of the couple, and gives help to both of them to live their lives faithfully together until death.

8. But marriage does not only exist for the two people concerned. Part of the reason why a permanent relationship is needed in marriage is for the provision of a home in which children may happily be brought up to share in the joys and sorrows of their parents, and to learn from them, and to support them.

9. This is part of the reason why the Church has taken a stand regarding certain methods of birth control, not because it wishes to take away from parents the right to decide how many children they can happily bring into the world, but because it sees the whole tendency in modern thinking as in some respects away from the interests of the child in the married relationship.

10. Christ in St John's Gospel was present at the Marriage Feast of Cana. His presence in any marriage will make that marriage both happy and fruitful.

> Fr Payton: The family that prays together
> stays together.
> Our Lady said to the servants at the Marriage Feast:
> Do whatever he (Christ) tells you.

Further discussion

Discuss the Church's attitude to divorce, sex outside marriage and contraception.

Scripture references

11.1 Song of Songs 5:2:8
11.4 Mark 10:1-12; Matthew 5:32
11.6 Ephesians 5:21-33
11.8 Psalms 127, 128
11.10 John 2:1-12

12. Friends of the Friends of God

1. Every society needs leadership, whether it is a large country like China or the USA, or whether it is a group at a disco or nightclub, where a natural 'leader' will often emerge. That leader will be good or bad insofar as he helps each individual in that group to feel part of the whole set-up, and insofar as he helps the group itself to grow and develop.

2. Christ our Lord, from the moment when he formed his community on earth, chose men who would be leaders, men whom he called the 'Twelve' - the same number as the twelve tribes of Israel. These he sent out to preach the Gospel, and to carry on his work.

3. These men were by no means perfect (the leader of the Twelve, Peter, denied Christ when he was arrested before his crucifixion), and came from ordinary professions. But still Christ said to them, 'As the Father sent me, so am I sending you'.

4. After the resurrection, the apostles became the leaders of the Church. Helped by the Holy Spirit they taught the new converts, led the celebration of Mass, and acted as judges within the Church in difficult situations.

5. But the Church was not meant to end with the first apostles. St Paul, one of the greatest apostles of them all, handed on the leadership of the new churches he had founded to people he called 'elders', laying hands on them as a sign of the Holy Spirit coming on them to help them. These 'elders' (presbyters) were the first leaders of the Church after the apostles, people we now call 'bishops' and 'priests'.

6. Since then, there have been thousands of priests and bishops ordained (that is, made priests by the laying on of hands). So much so, that there were over three thousand bishops present at the Second Vatican Council, from all over the world. The giving of 'holy orders' is another 'sacrament', a mystery where Christ is present, making a leader to represent him, to be 'another Christ'.

7. It is very important to realise that, although a priest has a high vocation, he is still very much human, going to confession just like everyone else, because he has often the very same failings as the people have who come to him to receive the forgiveness of Christ.

8. As time went on, the practice of priests not being married became a law in the Church in the West. In this way, the priest, and bishop, follows the way of Christ who was not married, in freeing himself even from good

human relationships, in order to be a father to the Christian community and to develop his life of personal prayer.

9. All Christians should regularly pray for priests, and especially for priests they know, so that the priest may be a good leader of the Christian community in the name of Christ, and a true friend of the friends of God. In this way, he will be worthy to take his place among the army of his brother priests, who have lived and sometimes died, in the service of God's people.

Further discussion

Discuss the organisation of the diocese; something about the bishop, the priests in the parish, other work which priests are called on to undertake.
Discuss the idea of 'ministry' with regard to priests and to lay people.

Scripture references

12.2 Matthew 10:1-5
12.5 Acts 14:23; 1 Peter 5:1-11
12.6 1 Timothy 1:18-20; 2 Timothy 1:6
12.9 1 Corinthians 7:32-35

13. Healing the Sick

1. In the life which we live on earth, sickness is one of the unfortunate things we fear most. It can take us away from our loved ones, and turn us from being active and responsible people into being totally dependent on someone else, almost like being an infant again.

2. In the Old Testament, sickness is treated as a great problem. In the story of Job, a good man suffers misfortune, crying out more than once, 'Why was I born at all, if my life is only like a prison?' But in the books written by the prophets, there is expressed the firm hope that one day God will save the sick, and the blind will see, the deaf hear, and the lame walk.

3. When Jesus came, he did so many miracles of healing that even those who did not accept him as the Messiah said, 'When the Messiah comes, will he do more miracles than this man has done?' We find that Jesus responded to human need, and in his pity healed the blind man who cried out, 'Jesus, Son of David, have pity on me'.

4. However, it is obvious that not all the people in Palestine at the time when Jesus was on earth were cured of their sickness. Some did not have faith, and so a cure

was not possible; and some were not around when Jesus
was passing by. And even those who were lucky enough
to be cured by him would still eventually have to submit
to the final sickness, death.

5. Therefore, the most important sickness of all was cured
by our Lord when he rose from the dead, what St Paul
called the 'last enemy' of the human race. We as Christians
know that death is only the gateway to a new life, in which
we will know and love God and each other completely.

6. After Pentecost, the apostles and other Christians did
as many remarkable things as Jesus himself had done
while on earth, healing men and women from serious
sickness such as paralysis, and from all kinds of sickness.
And since then, there have always been in the history of
the Christian Church, miracles of healing, often
associated with prayers of saints like Bernadette of
Lourdes, or with special manifestations of God's power
as in the charismatic renewal movement.

7. In connection with the healing of the sick, the Church
has a special sacrament whereby a person who is seriously
ill is anointed with holy oil. This is a sign to the sick
person that Christ is present as the divine Healer, and the
whole Church prays with faith as the Letter of St James
says, that he or she will recover to full health and strength.

8. However, just as in our Lord's day, not everyone who
is anointed with the Sacrament of the Sick will
necessarily recover; since all of us must die sometime. In
some cases, it is God's will to allow even a long illness,
as a way in which we can learn to love and to offer up our
sufferings to God in prayer for others. 'For', as St Paul
says, 'it is when I am weak that I am strong'.

9. Prayer of Thanksgiving at the Sacrament of the Sick:
Lord God, with faith in you, our brothers and sisters will
be anointed with this holy oil. Ease their sufferings and
strengthen them in their weakness. Through Christ our
Lord. Amen.

Finally, a short prayer for the sick person:

Our Lady, help of the sick, pray for him (or her).

Further discussion

Look through the rite of anointing the sick, read the
prayers carefully, and discuss the place of the Sacrament
in the Christian life.

Scripture references

13.2 Job 3:11
13.3 John 7:31; Mark 10:45-52
13.4 Mark 6:1-6
13.7 James 5:13-18
13.8 2 Corinthians 12:10

14. 'YOUR SINS ARE FORGIVEN'

1. 'Sin' is often treated as a joke in this day and age. But greed, unfaithfulness, hatred, pride, and selfishness are the cause of much of the unhappiness in the world today; and in a relationship between two people, offensive remarks and bad temper can cause a break in friendship only too easily.

2. We can never realise how wonderful God's forgiveness is, unless we can first understand how much God hates us doing what is wrong. He is our loving heavenly Father, and he expects us to be 'perfect', to be a true reflection of his own love, mercy, faithfulness and purity in our daily lives. And the problem is, none of us are.

3. However, as soon as we recognise our need for forgiveness, we are taking the first step to a change of heart, which we call technically 'conversion', 'repentance', or 'penance'. A change of heart, that is, from self to God.

4. The whole message of Jesus was one of forgiveness to those who were prepared to recognise that they were, in Jesus' own terms, 'sick'. 'I have not come to call the virtuous', he said, 'but sinners to repentance'. To the people who criticised him for allowing a woman of bad reputation to wash his feet with her tears and to dry them

with her hair, Jesus said, 'Her many sins are forgiven her, because she has loved much'. Such people knew the joy of the presence of Jesus and of friendship restored with him.

5. But Christ did not cease to be with us when he rose from the dead and went to be with his heavenly Father. He left his spirit of forgiveness to his Church, and particularly to his disciples, the Twelve, to whom he said, 'Whoever's sins you forgive, they are forgiven, and whoever's sins you retain, they are retained'.

6. This, then, is the basis of the sacrament of penance, the sacrament of forgiveness of sins; the continued presence of Christ with his Church. The priest does not come between us and God, but is a sign of Christ forgiving us when we are truly sorry, and when we are prepared to try our best not to offend God again. Like Christ himself, the priest will never refuse forgiveness (or 'absolution', as it is called) unless the person is putting a barrier up against God's forgiveness in some way, either by not being sorry, or by being really determined to refuse even to try to turn from what is wrong.

7. No Catholic is compelled to go to confession, and to receive the sacrament of forgiveness, unless he or she has committed a 'serious' sin against one of the Ten Commandments which we spoke of earlier. We should

confess our sins privately to God every day, and ask his forgiveness for our failings in love and holiness.

However, Catholics find the sacrament of forgiveness most helpful even when their consciences do not trouble them in a serious way, particularly through the encouragement of the priest's counsel and help. All that we say to a priest in the confessional, of course, is absolutely confidential, and will not be revealed even to the police.

Prayer for Absolution, said by the priest when we have made our confession:

God, the father of mercies, through the death and resurrection of his Son has reconciled the world to himself, and sent the Holy Spirit among us for the forgiveness of sins; through the ministry of the Church may God give you pardon and peace, and I absolve you from your sins, in the name of the Father, and of the Son, and of the Holy Spirit. Amen.

Further discussion

Go through the rite of reconciliation. Discuss some of the recommended readings. Discuss sin and its effect on us or on others. The social dimension of sin.

Scripture references

14.2 Leviticus 19:2; Matthew 5:48
14.3 Joel 2:12-17; Acts 2:37-41; Revelation 3:3
14.4 Matthew 9:13; Luke 7:47
14.5 John 20:23

15. THE CHARISMATICS

1. Each of us has some talent (music, do-it-yourself, knitting) which benefits not only ourselves and makes us feel we have achieved something, but which also gives enjoyment or help to someone else. A great cause of unhappiness in the world is when people feel their talents are not being used, or where their work is uninteresting or apparently futile.

2. Christ our Lord told the parable of the talents. The 'good' people who make their talents profitable are commended while the man who received only one talent is rebuked for not making anything out of his gift. Christ is saying that all of us, however useless we may feel ourselves to be, have been given gifts by God which we should try to use to the full.

3. But the Christian is not only given natural talents (sport or hobbies) but also spiritual gifts, to use for the benefit of the whole Church, the 'body of Christ'. Since each of us are members of that body, we have an essential part to play in the life of the Church.

4. The sacrament which gives us the strength and the help to develop these spiritual talents (and indeed our natural

talents when used in the service of God) is the sacrament of Confirmation. The bishop, or a priest designated by the bishop, lays his hands on the Christian, just as the apostles laid hands on the first Christians, and prays for the gift of the Holy Spirit to be given to them, as it was first given on the day of Pentecost.

5. Some of these gifts are quite extraordinary, like speaking in strange tongues, curing people of sickness, being able to see into the future (called 'prophecy') and casting out evil spirits. All these gifts have been present in the Church, and are particularly associated with people who are close to God.

6. But not only people with extraordinary talents are the Church's 'charismatics'. Priests receive the Holy Spirit at ordination, and their particular gift is to be leaders of the community in the name of Christ. Monks and nuns, called to live a life of prayer and contemplation, are filled with the desire to pray for their own salvation, and for ours. This strong desire is also a charism given by the Holy Spirit.

7. Another special gift from the Holy Spirit is the wish to give up everything for Christ, even things which are generally helpful to our life: property, freedom, and marriage. Thus, all down the centuries, men and women have taken vows of poverty (giving up the right to own

material goods), chastity (giving up the right to marriage), and obedience (giving up the right to make decisions about one's life, but doing simply what others in the community want, and so like Christ being servant to all).

8. As we saw earlier, marriage is a sacrament where the couple receive the help of Christ in their life together, not only for their own good, but also to build up the family of God. This is truly a vocation, just as much as those who take the 'vows', and for this the Holy Spirit is also given.

9. Finally, there are hundreds of spiritual talents which all exist for the building up of the body of Christ; mercy (giving up other things to nurse the sick, or feed the hungry); knowledge and faith (wanting to teach the Christian faith to others); reverence (filling us with the wish to be with God and to face life's difficulties in his presence).

10. And the greatest charism of all, as Paul said, is love, that same love which enabled Christ our Lord to die and rise again for us.

Scripture references

15.2 Matthew 25:14-30
15.2 1 Corinthians 12:4-11
15.4 Acts 19:1-7
15.10 1 Corinthians 13

16. THE LIFE OF PRAYER

1. We saw in the very first talk how the Catholic religion is essentially about developing friendship with God, our loving heavenly Father. One of the most important ways in which we express our friendship with another person is by talking to them, and listening to them. Prayer, according to St Augustine, may be described as 'conversation with God'.

2. Every Christian is strongly recommended to hold daily conversation with God, because we want to be conscious all the time of his loving presence, and ready to follow his wishes in the circumstances of our daily life.

3. Traditionally, Christians are encouraged to pray first thing in the morning and last thing at night, so that our first action of the day will be to say to God 'thy will be done', and the last action of the day will be to repose ourselves in the arms of the Father.

4. Morning and evening prayers (however long or short) are best done in the silence and secrecy of our own room. When we pray in secret, our heavenly Father will hear us in the personal secrecy of our hearts.

5. Our prayers should include simple praise of God for what he is and for what he has done for us; confession of our sins and failings, particularly those of the past day; prayers ('intercessions') for those we love, for those we find it difficult to love, and for our needs; and, most important of all, adoration of God who fills us with his presence and with his love.

6. As to the form of our prayer, we may use set prayers ('Our Father', 'Hail Mary', 'Glory be to the Father...' 'I confess...'), or quite informal talking to God. Most of us need a combination of set prayers and informal conversation with our heavenly Father, the set prayers helping us to formulate our thoughts, and informal conversation enabling us to express our personal ideas.

7. However, we must never forget that a most important element of prayer is simply being in the presence of God, and loving him without expressing any words at all. As the Curé d'Ars said, 'I looks at him, and he looks at me'. This form of simple adoration even goes beyond what we call 'meditation', which takes a religious idea and reflects upon it for a while.

8. Of course, not only morning and evening are for praying. It is good to take the opportunity of saying short prayers ('Hail Mary...', 'Lord Jesus Christ, Son of God

and Saviour, have mercy on me, a sinner') during the day, or to pay a visit to church and pray in the presence of Christ in the Blessed Sacrament.

9. A good practice when possible is to join in public prayer, either daily Mass, or other prayers in church. We should look upon the church as our home.

10. Finally, we must not be discouraged when God does not seem to answer our prayers. Sometimes, like any good Father, he says 'No' or 'Wait' to our requests, because finally he knows what is best for us, knowing as he does the whole plan.

   Lord, teach us to pray.

Further discussion

Discuss the various forms of public and private prayer in the Church.

Scripture references

16.4 Matthew 6:5-6; Daniel 5:11
16.7 Romans 8:26-27
16.8 Revelation 22:20 ('Come, Lord Jesus')
16.10 Luke 11:1

17. THE STORY OF THE CHURCH - I

1. Every individual feels the need to belong, to be part of a great family, or of a great enterprise. We love to be proud of past achievements of our country or family, and want to tell the story of these exploits to our friends and to our children. Just like the plants, human beings need to have strong roots.

2. As members of the Catholic Church, we have nearly two thousand years of history to recount, of which we are all a part. It is a fascinating story, as we look back to the 'rock from which we were hewn' (words spoken by the prophet Isiah, who lived centuries before the Church was founded); a story of saints and sinners, successes and failures, God working wonders through fallible human beings just like you and me. In its own way, a true miracle.

3. In the earliest days of the Church, when it grew extremely rapidly, there were more Jewish Christians than non-Jewish. The hero of the early days of the Church was Paul, who took the Gospel right across the known world to Rome.

Eventually, however, Jewish Christians became more and more dissatisfied with the lax attitude which Paul and other Christian leaders had towards the Jewish Law (Paul answering their objections by saying that the Law of circumcision was now fulfilled by Christian baptism). By the end of the first hundred years of Christianity, the Church had already become majority-Gentile rather than Jewish.

4. In the first two centuries Christianity was illegal, and many Christians became martyrs rather than worship the Emperor Caesar. Some of these martyrs were also great leaders and Christian thinkers, like Cyprian and Justine. Others of the 'early fathers' as they are called, like Chrysostom and Augustine, were not martyred, but wrote great works of theology (the scientific and systematic study of our faith in God) which we still read today.

5. After Christianity became a legal religion in the Roman Empire, the Catholic Church became very powerful in Europe, the Pope sometimes being more powerful than the Emperor as a political ruler, and the monks, who educated the people after the collapse of the old Roman Empire, became very wealthy and influential. But still, there was the desire to make the whole of life Christian, whether 'religion', 'politics', 'work', or 'play'.

6. In the Middle Ages, great saints like St Dominic and St Francis preached the Gospel wandering around the countryside with no money or possessions. In the universities, the greatest minds of the time like Thomas Aquinas and Duns Scotus (called 'scholastics') were lecturing and writing about the great problems of faith and life.

7. But the majority of the people apart from the clergy were illiterate, basing the religious life not upon solid preaching of Scripture, but upon legends of the saints; and the authorities in the Church were even more wealthy. Thus, later in the Middle Ages, men arose who challenged the whole authority of the Catholic Church, and said that new ideas were needed.

8. Already, a whole group of Christians in the East had separated from the Pope, calling themselves 'Orthodox', with almost the same beliefs as Catholics apart from belief in the final authority of the Bishop of Rome, the Pope. Sadly, this schism remains unhealed.

9. But now, a greater 'schism' or 'division' threatened the Church. In the early days of the Church, Christians debated whether Christ was truly God and Man, and even then, some Christians separated because some could not accept that Jesus was God (the Arians) and some could not accept that he was truly man (the Docetists). But a greater trouble still was brewing.

Scripture references

19.1 Revelation 2:5
19.2 Revelation 2:7; 1 Corinthians 10:1-5; Romans 12:1
19.3 Matthew 28:1
19.8 Luke 5:35

18. THE STORY OF THE CHURCH - II

1. In Britain, we feel ourselves to be very much a part of Western civilisation, which now has become very prosperous and highly developed in scientific and technological terms. The things which are so much a part of our everyday life in the West (television, electricity, railways, washing-machines) did not come out of the blue, but have grown up in European countries like Britain, France, and Germany which were all Catholic countries in the Middle Ages.

2. The Church encouraged scientific enquiry at first, one of the first great scientists being a Franciscan friar, Father Bacon. But a conflict soon arose when it seemed that some scientific ideas about the world did not square with the Bible; although now we are sure that there is no conflict between science and the Bible, because they are teaching different aspects of the truth.

3. But there was an even bigger conflict in Europe when a German friar called Martin Luther challenged the Pope's authority over the question of indulgences and, as time went on, Luther became even more bold, and found more and more of the German princes on his side. He challenged the need for the Church to interpret Scripture at all, saying that

the Bible alone was sufficient for faith. Thus eventually, Germany, Switzerland, and the Scandinavian countries, or at least large parts of them, accepted the 'protestant' religion.

4. In England, Henry Tudor VIII gave himself the title 'Head of the Church' in his own country, after Cardinal Wolsey had failed to persuade the Pope to give an annulment declaring invalid the king's marriage with Katherine of Aragon. In defiance of the Pope, Henry went ahead to marry Anne Boleyn, and the schism from Rome of the Church in England began.

5. Thus, by the middle of the sixteenth century, what was once Catholic Europe was in tatters, with Spain, Italy, Portugal and Ireland still remaining true to the old faith, but with the remaining countries now broken from Rome. Even other nations like France, still officially Catholic, were threatened with the possibility that they would be converted to the new religious ideas.

6. The first need was to reform and update the Catholic Church herself. This was done at the Council of Trent, which reformed the Mass, the training of priests, and deepened the understanding of Catholic doctrine. Thus arose a great era of what is called 'Counter Reformation', led by the Jesuit order and by the newly-trained secular priests, many of whom died a martyr's death for their faith.

7. From now on, there was a new spirit of free inquiry in Europe, which led to the great inventions which are now so much part of our lives, but which also led to the more scientific study of the Bible itself, by both Protestants and Catholics. There was also, however, growth in scepticism, and an increasing number of thinking persons who rejected the idea of supernatural religion.

8. In England, in the nineteenth century, there was a great revival of Catholicism in England, with a prominent Anglican theologian, John Henry Newman, becoming a convert to Catholicism. Great thinkers like Newman grappled with problems presented by atheism and agnosticism, and the Church prospered not only in Europe, but even more in the new colonies in Africa and in South America and in India.

9. In the twentieth century, marked by great changes due to technological progress, but also by incredible cruelty on a massive scale, the Christian Churches have come much closer together after the Second Vatican Council; and we pray with Christ that divisions may be healed, and 'that they all may be one...'

19. Living the Christian Life

1. All of us have the experience of starting some new venture with great enthusiasm, like a new hobby, but soon tiring of our first keenness. Even in the time of the writing of the New Testament, when the Church had only just begun, there were Christians who, in the words of the Book of Revelation, 'had lost their first love', and who were lukewarm in their faith, once accepted so eagerly.

2. But the true idea of the Christian faith is of our whole life offered in love and in service to God and to each other (Paul says, 'present your bodies as a living sacrifice to God'), and not of an emotional experience which comes on Sunday night and goes on Monday morning when we set out for school or work. The Bible often compares the Christian life to a pilgrimage through the desert, where courage, persistence, and 'stickability' through thick and thin is required of all of us, until we reach the 'promised land' of heaven.

3. As we plod steadily on through life as a Christian, the first essential is to pray regularly, both together with other Christians, and by ourselves. Above all, there is the need for weekly Mass, where we worship God together with the other members of our parish church, celebrating the

'first day of the week' when Mary Magdalene came to the tomb and found it empty, because Christ had risen.

4. Sunday above all should be a holiday (holy day), a time when we are refreshed physically and spiritually. In other words, we should enjoy it. The Church has never condemned legitimate pleasure on a Sunday (sport, theatre, etc.), but has always disapproved of work where that is not necessary. If a Catholic must work on a Sunday, then it is most advisable to have another day of rest, and to make provision for going to Mass at some time during the week.

5. The most important refreshment available to us is Holy Communion, which gives us the strength and help we need, in union with other Christians, as we travel through life. The Church only makes it a rule for Catholics to receive the body of Christ in communion once during the year, at Easter or thereabouts, when Christ rose from the dead three days after Good Friday, but we are encouraged to receive Communion every Sunday, or even more frequently if possible, to express and to deepen our union with Christ in the Father through the spirit.

6. But the Christian life is not all plain sailing, and, like Christ carrying his cross, sometimes we fall into sin. The rule is that Catholics go to confession by the end of the

year if they have a serious sin on their conscience; but this is only a minimum requirement, and we are recommended to go frequently to confession, to receive the sacrament of Christ's forgiveness, and to grow more like him in humility.

7. Also, to help us to become more like Christ, and to experience this 'change of heart' which we spoke of earlier, the Church appoints seasons of special preparation. Advent, preparing for Christmas, and Lent, preparing for Good Friday and Easter. To use this time of preparation well, and so to grow in our faith, hope and love, can be a great help in our Christian life.

8. During Advent and Lent, we are recommended to pray more, and also to 'fast', i.e. to deny ourselves some pleasure we do not really need, to help those less fortunate than ourselves by almsgiving, and to become more self-controlled. Paul compares a Christian to an athlete who goes into strict training, so that eventually he may win the race. Fasting is not a form of masochism, but a positive act of saying 'yes' to God, whereby we become masters of ourselves, and so servants of Christ, and of each other.

Further discussion

Discuss what being a Catholic means in practice.

20. QUESTIONS AND POINTS FOR DISCUSSION

1. What is the Catholic faith all about?
2. How do we know that God exists? Can we prove it?
3. Are the Ten Commandments still of value today?
4. Why is the Old Testament important to us as Christians?
5. Why do Catholics have such a strong devotion to Mary, the mother of Jesus?
6. Was Jesus only a teacher and miracle worker?
7. Why did Jesus die on the Cross, and suffer so much for us?
8. Why was Peter so important among the apostles?
9. What do Roman Catholics think about Christians of other denominations?
10. Why is the Pope so important for us? And the bishops?
11. What happens to us at our Baptism?
12. What do Catholics believe about the Eucharist?
13. Why does the Church not allow divorce between Christians?
14. Why is the Church so apparently strict about 'sex outside of marriage'?
15. What is the most important role of the priest in the Christian community?
16. Why do priests not marry? Could the law change in this respect?

17. Why does the sick and dying person so much need the help of the Church?
18. How often should a Catholic go to confession?
19. Why do people sometimes consecrate their whole lives to a religious order?
20. Has everyone an important job to do in the Church, whoever they are?
21. What should be done by us when we find prayer very difficult?
22. Does God always answer our prayers?
23. What can we do to help those people who are starving in the 'third world'?
24. Should a Christian be interested in politics?
25. What happens when we die?